IMAGES
of America

EL CERRITO

Huchiun Indians were the group of the Ohlone Indians who lived in the West Contra Costa County area. This sketch is part of a larger image drawn by Louis Choris, a Russian artist on the sailing ship *Rurik*. The *Rurik* departed St. Petersburg in 1815 on a Russian-sponsored expedition around the world and visited California in 1816. Choris's sketches of the people and places the *Rurik* visited are the only known images of a number of subjects. (Courtesy Bancroft Library, University of California, Berkeley; EC Historical Society [ECHS] collection.)

IMAGES
of America

EL CERRITO

El Cerrito Historical Society

ARCADIA
PUBLISHING

Published by Arcadia Publishing
Charleston, South Carolina

Library of Congress Catalog Card Number: 2005926997

For all general information contact Arcadia Publishing at:
Telephone 843-853-2070
Fax 843-853-0044
E-mail sales@arcadiapublishing.com
For customer service and orders:
Toll-Free 1-888-313-2665

Visit us on the Internet at www.arcadiapublishing.com

CONTENTS

ACKNOWLEDGMENTS

The editorial committee of the El Cerrito Historical Society is indebted to several people for the completion of this book.

First to Louis L. Stein, who collected photographs and information in the East Bay, including El Cerrito, which he generously shared with various historical groups. Second, to Mervin Belfils, who cared for the Stein collection and added much of his own over the years. His wife, Ruth, gave the entire collection to the historical society for use and safekeeping. Mr. Belfils wrote articles for our bulletin, and many of the captions in this book are his.

We are very grateful to the many individuals who have generously donated photographs from their own personal collections to the society. The large volume of photographs in our files required us to be selective in choosing which could clearly portray the history of our city.

Finally, without the energy and countless hours of personal contacts and organization of materials by our member Tom Panas, this book would not have been published.

INTRODUCTION

Before the Spanish explorations of the San Francisco Bay region, many different groups of Ohlone Indians inhabited the Bay Area. Today, reminders of these people are still found in the shell mounds, mortar holes, and rock art they left behind. The Spanish explorations into California began with the expedition of Gaspar de Portola in 1769. After setting up a base in San Diego, the expedition departed for the Port of Monterey. Pedro Fages, whom Portola had assigned to govern Alta California, then set out in spring 1772 with Fr. Juan Crespi and 12 soldiers to explore the eastern shore of San Francisco Bay. This was the first Spanish exploration of what are now the counties of Santa Clara, Alameda, and Contra Costa. On March 27, 1772, they camped on the bank of a creek opposite the Golden Gate. They named the hill "Serrito [sic] de San Antonio" (cerrito meaning "little hill"), which became the source of the name for the city of El Cerrito.

At the time of the Mexican revolution, the area now known as Contra Costa County was used as grazing land for sheep and cattle belonging to Mission Dolores in San Francisco. Francisco Castro, a former soldier at the San Francisco presidio and alcalde of the pueblo of San Jose, had been a member of an exploration party through the area. On April 15, 1823, he received a provisional grant for approximately four square leagues (19,394.40 acres) from Governor Arguello. The grant became known as Rancho San Pablo. It was finalized in 1834.

This grant included all the land between San Pablo Creek (on the north), Cerrito Creek (on the south), the bay (on the west), and the top of the ridge separating Wildcat Canyon from today's El Cerrito and Richmond (on the east). Francisco Castro took possession of an old mission dwelling on this rancho near the present town of San Pablo and made extensive revisions. In 1839, one of his sons, Victor Ramon Castro, chose a spot along the creek at the southern edge of his father's sprawling rancho to build the hacienda that today we refer to as the Castro Adobe. It was here that Victor Castro lived with his wife, Luisa, and their family.

Luisa was the daughter of Ignacio Martinez, whose land grant was adjacent to the north end of the Castro land grant. Victor Castro raised cattle, fruit, grains, and vegetables on his rancho. He also owned a schooner launch and a whaleboat, which he kept at Point Isabel and at the mouth of Cerrito Creek. The two-story adobe that the Castro family built near Cerrito Creek stood for 117 years, until it burned to the ground just before construction started on El Cerrito Plaza in April 1956. A brass plaque on the west side of El Cerrito Plaza now marks the site of Castro Adobe.

William F. Rust, a journeyman blacksmith who came to America from Hanover, Germany, in 1877 at the age of 20 was considered one of the founders of El Cerrito, even though others lived in the area before he did. Rust arrived in 1883 and settled in San Pablo, a regular stopping place on the road between Oakland and Martinez. After briefly returning home to his native Germany, he built a blacksmith shop on the main road (now San Pablo Avenue) between Oakland and San Pablo, just north of the Alameda–Contra Costa County line.

Victor Castro owned all the land in this part of the county and leased a great deal of it to tenant farmers. Rust rented a plot of ground from one of Victor Castro's tenant farmers, H. Albertson, for $20 a year. Rust subsequently agreed to give Victor Castro an additional $5 a year. Rancho San Pablo was excellent farmland, and Rust developed a good business making farm implements.

From 1900 to 1901 there was a post office named Schmidtville in the area of Schmidt Lane. The 1906 San Francisco earthquake sent a flood of refugees to the East Bay, some of whom eventually took up residence in the county line area and near Stege Junction (the area near the intersection of San Pablo and Potrero Avenues). In 1909, a post office was established in William Rust's store, Rust was named postmaster, and the post office was named "Rust" after him. On

August 23, 1917, after a spirited contest, the unincorporated areas of Rust and Stege Junction voted on incorporation: 158 votes for and 131 against. The resulting new city was named El Cerrito. Starting with an estimated population of 1,400 in 1917, the area reached a population of 3,852 in 1930 and 7,000 in 1940. During World War II, the population jumped to nearly 17,000.

During the 1930s and early 1940s, the community was known throughout the West for its casinos, poker parlors, and dog racing. The Castro Adobe housed one of the well-known gambling spots and clubs of the time. In 1945, a group of citizens who wanted to be proud of the city in which they lived and who wanted to create a desirable place to raise families formed a group known as the Good Government League. They adopted the slogan "The City of Homes" and then set about to build a city that would live up to that slogan. The Good Government League—campaigning on a platform of clean, efficient government—was successful in recalling three city council members and electing an entirely new city council at the same time that an increase in permanent housing was beginning to make El Cerrito truly a city of homes.

The first major acts of the new city council were to outlaw draw poker and to embark on a vigorous enforcement campaign against all gambling. Two years later, the council-manager form of government was adopted to aid in streamlining and reorganizing the city. Over the next decades, city council members and administrators put in motion vigorous plans to improve streets, build parks, and enhance city services, all of which led to the family-oriented city that El Cerrito is today.

One

BEFORE 1900

This view looks south toward Albany Hill from Road Eight (now Central Avenue) about 1861. The small knoll on the right was later the location of the Judson Powder Company, where there was a large explosion in 1905. (Courtesy Louis L. Stein, ECHS collection.)

Don Victor Ramon Castro stands in front of his adobe in 1895. Castro made his home for many years at what we now refer to as the Castro Adobe, which he started to build in 1839. Two hundred Indians worked to build the adobe. It was located at the present site of the El Cerrito Plaza shopping center. The adobe grounds included a number of buildings and a large orchard. The adobe burned to the ground April 20, 1956. (Courtesy ECHS collection.)

This view of the Castro Adobe shows the fountain in front and the main buildings. The adobe was said to have been one of the most gracious of all the Mexican haciendas. It was the locale used by Bret Harte in his 1857 play *Two Men of Sandy Bar*, written after he had been Castro's guest at the adobe. (Courtesy ECHS collection.)

Castro was born March 6, 1820 and died May 5, 1900. His wife, Luisa Martinez, was the daughter of Don Ignacio Martinez, whose land grant was adjacent to the north end of the Castro land grant. Luisa gave birth to six children, only two of whom survived. Point Isabel was named after one of his daughters. (Courtesy Louis L. Stein, ECHS collection.)

Students and teacher Clara Chichester pose in front of the Castro School building sometime before the turn of the century. The building was originally located near the county line on the grounds of the Castro Adobe (hence the name) and later moved up San Pablo Avenue near the present site of St. John's Catholic Church. In fact, the building was later sold to the church and became the first St. John's church. (Courtesy Richmond Museum of History.)

Looking west across San Pablo Avenue from near Road Four (now Fairmount Avenue) at the blacksmith establishment of William (Wilhelm) Rust. Rust's wife, Lina, is sitting in the carriage with their son Herman in her arms. From left to right are Wilhelm Rust, his son William, employee Joe Lager, and two unidentified men. The Rust residence can be seen at the far right. (Courtesy Louis L. Stein, ECHS collection.)

Two

1900–1909

Around 1905, this haying crew worked a field near the Sunset View Cemetery. The boy at the left is Harry F. Lonseale, the half-brother of Albert Wilson. The woman sitting on the hay is Lizzie Davis. Behind her is her husband, Eddie Davis. (Courtesy ECHS collection.)

William (Wilhelm) Rust, stands with his daughter-in-law Ivy Rust. She was married to Wilhelm's oldest son, William. The young boy is Robert Davis Rust, Wilhelm's grandson and the son of Ivy and William Rust. (Courtesy ECHS collection.)

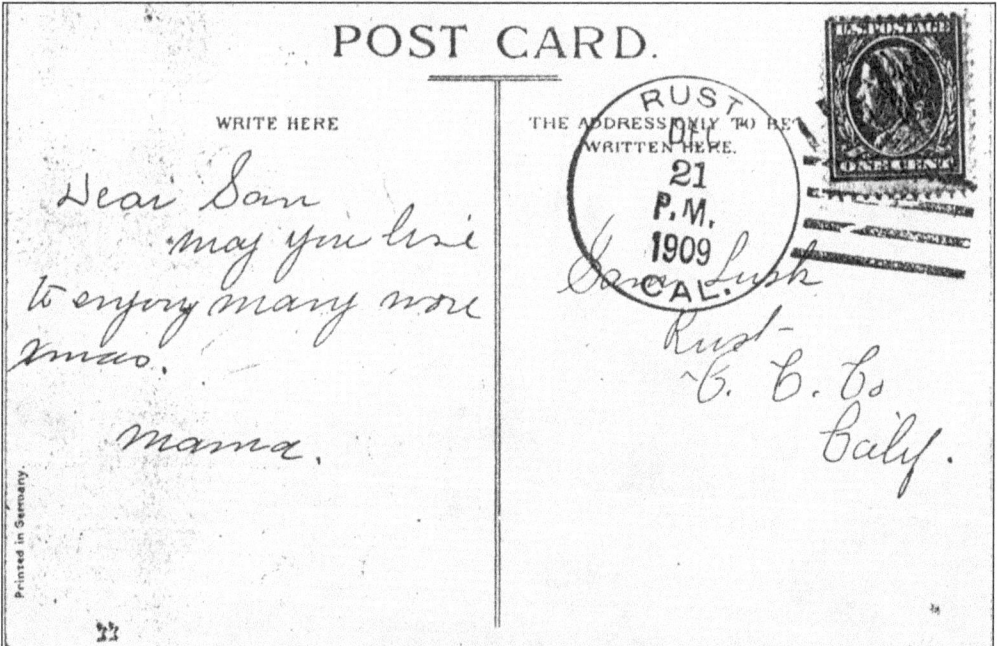

This postcard has a "Rust, Cal" postmark. Note the one-cent stamp and the third line of the address ("C. C. Co.") This postcard was mailed from and to Rust. (Courtesy Umbraco family, ECHS collection.)

The Seven Mile House that once stood at Fairmount and San Pablo Avenues is now the site of the Mechanics Bank. The fence behind the willow trees runs along Fairmount Avenue. Posing at the rear of the house are, from left to right, the nurse (unidentified), Louis Davis, Mary Davis, Grandpa (John H.) Davis, Grandma Davis, Emma Davis, and George Speck. (Courtesy ECHS collection.)

This photograph shows William Rust's hardware store and other shops on San Pablo Avenue near Fairmount Avenue, at the approximate location of today's Pastime Hardware. The post office is on the left of the hardware store, and the Rust's house is on the right. Pictured, from left to right, are William Rust, Miss Alice McCarthy, and Rust's wife, Lina. (Courtesy Louis L. Stein, ECHS collection.)

This streetcar, owned by the Cornel Rheem Company, connected to the main line along San Pablo Avenue at Stege Junction (Potrero and San Pablo). Some of the cars on this line branched off and ran along the creek to Eastshore Park and property later owned by Anna Soldavini at 980 South Forty-seventh Street. From left to right are ? Uttervack, ? Delani, Mervin McNalley, and ? Soldavini. (Courtesy ECHS collection.)

On August 16, 1905, there was a major explosion at the Judson Powder Company, which was located on the north side of Albany Hill. The two lines through the picture are said to be where the explosion cracked the lens in the camera. The nitroglycerin house exploded, killing two men. (Photograph by Charles Johnson; courtesy ECHS collection.)

James Lipp (sometimes called "Blind Jim") and his dog Tippy pose at San Pablo Avenue and the county line. This structure was built at the end of the Oakland streetcar line in 1906 by Mayor Davies of Oakland. (Courtesy ECHS collection.)

On San Pablo Avenue at County Line, Streetcar No. 246 (on the left) is parked on the side for cars to and from Oakland. The Santa Fe emblem on the car indicates the car serves the Santa Fe station at 40th and San Pablo. Streetcar No. 53 (on the right) is on the side for cars to and from Richmond. Passengers had to pay an extra fare to go beyond this point in either direction. There is a newsstand and lunch counter in the middle of San Pablo Avenue. The small building on the left is the Boulevard Gardens real estate office of Schmidt Skilling Company. The large building is a rooming house and saloon that was once owned by Louis Hagen. Hagen operated the rooming house while Fred Munday ran the saloon. The sign on the pole is a political card promoting a candidate for supervisor. (Courtesy ECHS collection.)

This 1906 photograph of the Henderson Tapscott tract looks down from Norvell Street toward the bay. Point Isabel is at the right of the picture, with the powder company building visible on the Point. At San Pablo and Central Avenues (near the trees) is the Six Bells building. The Breneman building, visible farther to the north on San Pablo Avenue, was demolished in 1963. The Rube Curry building is the leftmost building on the far side of the Santa Fe tracks, which run left to right through the cluser of houses. (Courtesy ECHS collection.)

George Barber was El Cerrito's first city marshal. He also functioned as the tax and license collector, dog catcher, street inspector, and building inspector. The George Barber home at 729 Richmond Street was built in 1908. (Courtesy ECHS collection.)

Ellen Colford (on the right) and a friend pose on a footbridge over the north fork of Cerrito Creek, which in this area ran generally between Central and Lincoln Avenues. The bridge from which the picture was taken is believed to be on Richmond Street between Central and Lincoln Avenues. The view is generally east, with the Colford family house on Norvell Street in the background. (Courtesy Colford-Smith family, ECHS collection.)

Tony Marsala stands beside a wagon at what is now the southwest corner of Central Avenue and Liberty Street. Looking north up Liberty Street, the three houses on the right are in the 500 block (between Central Avenue and Willow Street). Marsala later had a store at the corner of Central Avenue and Richmond Street. The wagon's lettering reads, "Tony Marsala, 411 Central Ave., Rust, Calif." The peak on the hill in the distance behind the wagon is Murietta Rock, near Arlington Avenue and Cutting Boulevard. (Courtesy ECHS collection.)

St. John's Catholic Church on San Pablo Avenue is where Fr. Anthony Heneghan, the assistant father at Berkeley's St. Ambrose Catholic Church, held services and administered the sacraments. This building had previously been the Castro School, on the grounds of the Castro Adobe. Murietta Rock is visible in the distance. (Courtesy ECHS collection.)

Pictured in front of Stege School are, from left to right, (first row) John Hintz, Carrie Nisson, Winnie Mills, Alma Hoffman, Ellen Smith (later Mrs. Regalia), and teacher Mrs. Watrus; (second row) Eddie Matson, George Bailey, Cherry Bailey, Harry Davis, and Arthur Avila; (third row) Mary Joseph, Grace Young, and Roy Darling; (fourth row) Clifford Fallon, Emilie Renkwitz (later Mrs. Reinecker), Harold Fallon, and Hazel Ross. (Courtesy ECHS collection.)

This Fairmont School class includes, from left to right, (front row) unidentified, Edna Brennan, Bianca Roberti, Mary Marsala, Theresa Guiffre, Apperson Wright, Teddy Ross, Sarah Molica, Raymond Bowers (son of Mrs. Bowers), and two unidentified children; (second row) two unidentified, Georgia Hinds, two unidentified, Viva Josephson, Art Peralta, Joe Marsala, Pearl Wright, Ina Josephson, and Izzy Perman; (third row) two unidentified, ? Comaroti, Dorothy Schaefer, Lucille Allinio, Katy Perman, Julia Domingo, Tony Molica, John Domingo, Mark Cheeseman, Hershel Klase, two unidentified, Florence Domingo, Herman Stark, Dorothy Morrill, and Eugene Charling; (fourth row) unidentified, Clara Gustafson, Evelyn Keller, Thurston Stark, Elma Klase, George Schaefer, two unidentified, and teacher Mrs. Bowers. (Courtesy ECHS collection.)

This group enjoyed their bottles at Lafayette Park in 1905. Lafayette Park was at the northeast corner of Blake Street and San Pablo Avenue and was a very popular place for parties and dancing. Pete Soldavini is at the right, with his arm on the bar. (Courtesy ECHS collection.)

The Al Bigley home, pictured, was demolished in October 1968. The house was at 620 Lexington Avenue. At the very top of the hills, above the right side of the roof, the Bates and Borland Quarry can be seen. A tramway brought the quarried rock down to a crusher and bunkers (or gravel piles) located at what is today's Cerrito Vista Park. Just above the left side of the roof, the end of the tramway and the gravel pile can be seen. (Courtesy Louis L. Stein, ECHS collection.)

The view northeast from Central and San Pablo Avenues in 1906 shows streetcar tracks on San Pablo Avenue. The Bates and Borland Quarry (now Camp Herms) at the top of the hill is visible, as is the gravel pile at the bottom of the tramway (located at the site of today's Cerrito Vista Park). The tract office was later moved to the corner of Liberty and Willow Streets. (Courtesy ECHS collection.)

At the lower right of this image is the intersection of Lexington and Lincoln Avenues. The fence line is along the Santa Fe tracks. The building on the left beyond the tracks is the Methodist church in the 500 block of Richmond Street at the corner of Willow Street. (Courtesy ECHS collection.)

This is a view of El Cerrito from Albany Hill. The Victor Castro Adobe is just north of Cerrito Creek, which runs west in the lower right corner of the photograph. A streetcar is visible on San Pablo Avenue, and the building on San Pablo Avenue with the cupola on top is Hagen's County Line Saloon. The large building near the top of the hill at the right of the picture is believed to be John Balra's dairy. (Courtesy Louis L. Stein, ECHS collection.)

Tony Regalia's Saloon, at the southwest corner of Potrero and San Pablo Avenues, is pictured in 1903. The wheel of Lottman's beer wagon is partly visible on the left. Henry Lottman drove the keg wagon for Raspillar Brewery of Berkeley. The property was owned by Henry Kleese before Tony Regalia purchased it. In front of the door, from left to right, are Frank Lottman, Pete Soldavini, and Tony Regalia. (Courtesy ECHS collection.)

The Bottini residence at 11476 San Pablo Avenue was built in 1902. The Bottini family had a dairy farm near MacDonald Avenue in the early 1900s. From left to right are unidentified, Giovanne, Susie, and Adeline Bottini. (Courtesy ECHS collection.)

Three

1910–1919

The Stag House was built at the corner of Burlingame and San Pablo Avenues by Mrs. Johnson, around 1912. Burlingame Avenue was originally Coalinga Boulevard, but the street name was changed very early. The inn's name was later changed to the La Vyra Inn by Charles and Vyra Kerr, as Mrs. Kerr's stage name was La Vyra. The La Vyra Inn was one of the better known "hot pillow" houses in El Cerrito. It is now called the Hillside Inn. (Courtesy ECHS collection.)

Frank Lewis rides high on the grounds of the Bates and Borland Quarry (the site of today's Cerrito Vista Park). Visible at the right is a small part of the tramway that brought rock down to the crusher at that site from the company's quarry above Arlington Avenue. Frank has a rope, leather chaps, and all the other gear a well-equipped cowboy would need before venturing out into the wild El Cerrito hill country. (Courtesy ECHS collection.)

Here is one of the trucks owned by Lewis and McDermott Wholesale Butchers. William Lewis left the business in its early days, but was so highly regarded by the McDermott family that the Lewis family name remained associated with the business for many years. (Courtesy ECHS collection.)

The Lewis and McDermott slaughterhouse, seen here from El Dorado Street looking south toward Albany, was run by William Lewis and Frank McDermott. The slaughterhouse's location was near today's intersection of Central Avenue and Belmont Street. (Courtesy ECHS collection.)

A young Joseph Lewis stands in the lush meadow just north of Albany hill and south of Central Avenue. This area was very swampy in the early days. Not only was there a tidal influence (as Cerrito Creek met San Francisco Bay just west of here), but three forks of Cerrito Creek met in this area. The sheep in the photograph will have an appointment at his father's place of business, just out of view on the left, in the not-too-distant future. (Courtesy ECHS collection.)

The Talt family gathers for Easter dinner in the dining room at the Castro Adobe. The Talt family occupied the Castro Adobe and grounds in the years after the turn of the century, and they had a very successful chicken ranch there. This one-of-a-kind photograph turned up after a very lengthy search initiated by a comment made by George Pryde, himself a first-generation member of the pioneering Pryde family. George's comment was to the effect of, "You know, there was a Talt family who had a chicken farm at the foot of Fairmount Avenue." (Courtesy LaReau family, ECHS collection.)

This is an early view west from approximately where today's Potrero Avenue and Navellier Street meet. Mt. Tamalpais is visible across the bay. The house in the foreground is unidentified. Further west is the Santa Fe right-of-way. The large building beyond the Santa Fe and above the house is the Grand Central building at Potrero and San Pablo Avenues. The boxy, two-story building further out Potrero is Stege School. Following the Santa Fe tracks to the right, the large grove of trees is Lafayette Park. Blake Street was the southern boundary of Lafayette Park. The very small building just northeast of where the Santa Fe crossed Blake Street is the "shelter shed" Santa Fe built for passengers at the "station" the Santa Fe originally called Dwight and later renamed Cerrito. (Courtesy Louis L. Stein, ECHS collection.)

Pictured are Albert, Emilie, and Marie Renkwitz— the grandfather, mother, and grandmother of Elsa Reinecker. The Reineckers had a chicken ranch at the foot of the El Cerrito hills, southeast of the intersection of Potrero Avenue and Navellier Street (where the "Wildwood" development is located today). (Courtesy Lent family, ECHS collection.)

Muriel Talt smiles for the photographer from a donkey cart at the Talt family's "humble" abode, the old Castro Adobe. The family had a large chicken ranch here for a number of years. (Courtesy LaReau family, ECHS collection.)

Here is Molica's fruit and vegetable wagon, as viewed from the upstairs porch of Dr. Breneman's home north of Central Avenue, near Avila Street, at 525 San Pablo Avenue (10135 San Pablo Avenue after the renumbering). Eula Breneman (who later married Joe Staley) selects fruit and vegetables from Molica's wagon. Across San Pablo Avenue is the George Conlon property on Kearney Street, south of Lincoln Avenue. Kearney Street is the dusty trace just above the cows, running parallel to San Pablo Avenue. The Breneman building was demolished in 1963. (Courtesy ECHS collection.)

Leon and Lena Fry enjoy the sunshine near the corner of Lassen Street and San Pablo Avenue. They lived close by. The trees and hedge on the left are the entrance to the Castro Adobe. The building is the County Line Saloon. (Courtesy ECHS collection.)

Just below the quarrying operation of the Bates and Borland Quarry (where Arlington Park is today), a goat pulls Evelyn Keller. The rock quarried here rode down a funicular tramway to Bates and Borland's crusher, at the site of today's Cerrito Vista Park. Evelyn later married quarry worker Earl L. Morrill. Today's boy scout camp above Arlington Park, Camp Herms, occupies the hole left behind by the quarrying operations. (Courtesy ECHS collection.)

This photograph shows the corner of Road Four (now Fairmount Avenue) and San Pablo Avenue. The man is believed to be Lester Zahniser. The Seven Mile House (seven miles from downtown Oakland) was built in 1879 and owned by John H. Davis. The house at left was moved to Central Avenue and Kearney Street and became the Shoute family home. (Courtesy ECHS collection.)

Minna Voges, who came from Germany in 1902, married William (Wilhelm) Rust in 1918. Rust's first wife was Lina Wagner. They were married in 1886 and she died in 1914. Lina and Wilhelm had two sons, William and Herman. (Courtesy ECHS collection.)

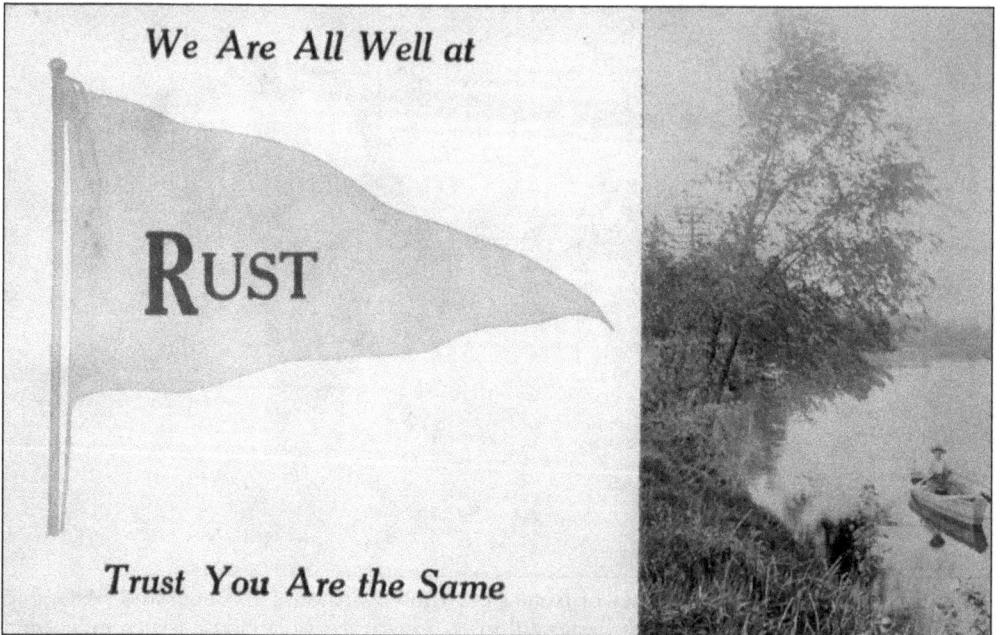

Postcards were very popular in the early part of the century, and just about every town worth its stuff had at least one card. The citizens of Rust were certainly not about to be outdone. (Courtesy Jackson family, ECHS collection.)

The Rust Post Office was located inside William Rust's hardware store. Rust was, of course, the postmaster. The word "hardware" can be seen on the store windows. (Commercial Art Company photograph; courtesy Umbraco family, ECHS collection.)

El Cerrito's first city council (1917) included, from left to right, (first row) George F. Scott, treasurer; Henry Wildgrube, attorney; Grace Castner, clerk; and Peter Larsen; (second row) Phillip A. Lee; John Sandvick; Kirk E. Gray, mayor; and George W. Adams. (Courtesy ECHS collection.)

This photograph looks west across the Santa Fe tracks, from Central Avenue and Richmond Street. (Courtesy ECHS collection.)

The Hutchinson Quarry was started in 1900 here at Navellier Street and Schmidt Lane. The Edward Temperli home is on the left, along with a platform for a dance floor. The surveyors near the pole are believed to be Ross Calfee and crew. The bunkers for the quarry are at the right.

This is a view looking west from the Hutchinson Quarry site at the top of Schmidt Lane. The dance floor at the Temperli house is visible in the foreground, as is a gondola sitting on the part of the Santa Fe spur that ran into the quarry's tailings area. The hothouses of the Figone Nursery are visible further down Schmidt Lane. The hill on Point Isabel, before it was leveled by Santa Fe Land Development, is clearly visible. Richmond Annex (not to mention most of El Cerrito) is almost all flowers and fields. (Courtesy ECHS collection.)

Very little of the hill has been quarried at this date. Today El Cerrito's corporation yard is on the right and the recycling center is on the left. (Courtesy ECHS collection.)

Dr. Joseph T. Breneman, the first doctor in El Cerrito, poses with his family outside their home at 525 San Pablo Avenue. In addition to serving as the family home, the house was his office for a time and the area's library for 10 years. From left to right are (second row) his four daughters Fay, Frances, Eula, and Hazel; and his wife Fannie. The two stars in the window indicate two sons who were serving in World War I. (Courtesy ECHS collection.)

At the Fairmont School, teacher Mrs. Hough (Huff) poses with her students, from left to right, (first row) unidentified, Albert Wilson, Apperson Wright, unidentified, Ralph Renfree, Tony Molica, two unidentified, Fritz Lotter, Vernon Crespan, unidentified, Archie Zahniser, Erwin Markain, Mervin Brennan, and unidentified; (second row) Sarah Molica, Mabel Carrling, Emma Gobba, Ida Roberti, Mary Marsala, Bianca Roberti, four unidentified, Erma Roberti, and three unidentified; (third row) Teddy Ross, May Renfree, Edna Brennan, Bernice Carpenter, unidentified, Josephine Stark, Viva Josephson, Christina Shoute, Arthur Peralta, Ina Josephson, Rosetta Hall, unidentified, Kenneth Guide, Keneln Younge, and Manual Swartz. (Courtesy ECHS collection.)

The Modern Order of Praetorians baseball team won the Bay Area championships in both 1914 and 1915. Pictured, from left to right, are (first row) Harold Otterman, Louis Davis, and Andy Jackson; (second row) D. Newell, Chet Bertolacci, S. Sharkenetti, Tom Moccicane, Charles Bertoli, Rose Dorrett, and Stanley Emery. (Courtesy ECHS collection.)

Erwin Lotter and a friend hold still for the camera at the Keller Ranch, which was located between Contra Costa Drive and Arlington Avenue in about the 1100 block, north of the old Bates and Borland tramway. (Courtesy Lotter family, ECHS collection.)

The Grand Central building at the northwest corner of San Pablo Avenue and Potrero Avenue was owned by Mr. Lavigne (standing on the left and wearing a vest). On his left, leaning against the post, is his son Joe Lavigne. Dr. Breneman's office was upstairs on the right in this building for a time; his name can be seen on an upstairs window. This building was demolished in September 1967. (Courtesy ECHS collection.)

Frank Weeks is behind the counter of John Morris's store at 415 Richmond Street. John Morris leans on the counter. The twin boys on chairs are Donald and Ronald Raymer. (Courtesy ECHS collection.)

The Annex Grocery store on the corner of Panama and San Pablo Avenues was run by Serafino Chiovaro. Pictured out front are, from left to right, Serafino, daughter Christina, wife Nunzia, and granddaughter Prudence. The Chiovaros moved to the East Bay because of the 1906 earthquake and settled in El Cerrito. (Courtesy Hansen family, ECHS collection.)

For many years, the Grand Central building stood at "Stege Junction" on the corner of San Pablo and Potrero Avenues. In those days, the East Shore and Suburban's trolley main line went up San Pablo Avenue from the county line to MacDonald Avenue and then turned west to reach downtown Richmond and the San Rafael ferry. A branch line was later built that ran out Potrero to the town of Stege and then up Pullman (now Carlson) to rejoin the Main Line at Twenty-third Street. The name "Stege Junction" became associated with this part of town. Out Potrero Avenue, the boxy structure between the streetcar poles is Stege School, and in the distance is a streetcar. (Burg Brothers photograph; courtesy of Louis L. Stein, ECHS collection.)

Ed Phipps stands in front of the bar he owned at the northeast corner of Fairmount and San Pablo Avenues. Phipps was the stepfather of William Hinds, El Cerrito's first fire chief. (Courtesy St. John family, ECHS collection.)

Henry Timm's saloon, the Palm Garden, was at the corner of San Pablo Avenue and Schmidt Lane. The sign says "American Brewery Depot." (Courtesy ECHS collection.)

Here is the Panama Pacific Saloon, on the east side of San Pablo Avenue between Manila and Madison Avenues. This photograph was taken looking east. Murietta Rock can be seen in the distance. (Courtesy ECHS collection.)

This photograph looks south down San Pablo Avenue. The building on the right side is at the corner of Jefferson and San Pablo Avenues. On the southwest corner is the saloon of Joe Villalobos. The building on the left (east) side of San Pablo Avenue between Manila and Madison Avenues is the Panama Pacific Saloon. (Courtesy ECHS collection.)

Josephine Stark, whose father worked at the Bates and Borland Quarry on Moeser Lane, poses in a field of lupine in the El Cerrito Hills. Old-timers uniformly recall that the El Cerrito fields and hills were covered with flowers in the spring. One 90-year-old-plus former resident who moved to the East Coast around 1930 and has never been able to return to El Cerrito asked the question in 2004, "Is El Cerrito still all fields?" (Courtesy Johnson family, ECHS collection.)

This view from Blake Street and San Pablo Avenue looks up Blake Street and then south along the hills. San Pablo runs toward Oakland, and the tracks visible on San Pablo carried the East Shore and Suburban Railroad, which one could ride (with a transfer at county line) from the San

This photograph looks east over the hothouses of the Japanese nurserymen, whose businesses were the main economic enterprise in the northwest part of El Cerrito and the adjoining part of Richmond. About 15 different nurseries once covered this area; today only remnants of the Sakai and Oishi nurseries remain. (Courtesy Richmond Library, ECHS collection.)

Rafael ferry all the way to downtown Oakland. The building on the right is the Grand Central building at San Pablo and Potrero Avenues. (Courtesy ECHS collection.)

The sign on Naggaro Moro's store proclaims "Plumbing & Tinning" and "Kitchen Utensils." From left to right are Naggaro's wife, Maria; Naggaro; and his two daughters, Jennie and Josephine. The business was established and the store was built in 1903. (Courtesy Soldavini family, ECHS collection.)

Louie and Ida Navellier stand in front of the Ernest Navellier home on the east side of Navellier Street (in those days Blake Street), between Donal and Manila Avenues. Louie was born in this house in 1899. His sister Ida married and became Ida Bray. The Navellier family came to the Richmond area in 1892. (Courtesy ECHS collection.)

The Tom Pickles house on 630 Richmond Street is pictured in 1911. Bells hanging in the window indicate it is Christmas time. The Bates and Borland Quarry is visible at the left near the top of the hills. Note that compared to today there are few trees on the hills. (Courtesy ECHS collection.)

Mrs. Moro stands in front of the family store. The year is 1913. In the two years that have passed since the photograph from the previous page, electricity has arrived. The building itself makes good reading. (Courtesy ECHS collection.)

This view from Richmond Annex looks up Schmidt Lane to the Hutchinson Quarry site at the top of Schmidt Lane. To the left, above the Hutchinson Quarry, is the Bates and Borland Quarry. On the right side of the picture is their gravel pile. The rock came down a tramway from their quarry above Arlington (at the site of today's Camp Herms). The bottom end of the tramway

can be seen leading down to the gravel pile. Also visible are segments of the tramway that lead up to the quarry. The area north of Schmidt Lane is being farmed, as rows of crops are visible. William C. Lewis is in the foreground, and there is a young orchard on the left. (Courtesy Collier family, ECHS collection.)

A car has just crossed the Santa Fe tracks near San Pablo Avenue and heads east on Hill Street toward Allen Street (now Lexington Avenue). (Courtesy ECHS collection.)

Fairmont School (pictured) burned down in October of 1924. A new school was built in its place, and that school was subsequently remodeled. The dirt road in the foreground is Eureka Avenue. Murietta Rock is visible in the distance. (Courtesy ECHS collection.)

Four

1920–1929

In a typical scene from earlier times, the McDonald family is "camping out" in a tent near the place where they are building their house. When finished, it was the first house the family ever lived in where they had indoor plumbing. The house was on Central Avenue near Clayton Avenue. (Courtesy Collins family, ECHS collection.)

The father and son Lewis team, plus the hired hands, have been successful in gathering plenty of hay to feed the animals at the Lewis and McDermott slaughterhouse. William C. Lewis is on the left, the hired hands are in the middle, and Frank Lewis is on the right. (Courtesy ECHS collection.)

This photograph looks south on San Pablo Avenue from near Fairmount Avenue, just after a big rain and wind storm. The building at the extreme right is Judge MacKinnon's office, which had also been used for collecting water bills and as a real estate office. The building at the corner of Lassen Street was a cabinet shop and had been run by Frank Walsh and also by Mr. Hale. The barber sign is for a shop run by a female barber. At the far left is B. F. Denton's Feed and Fuel store. The fourth building from the left is Minor's grocery store, and beyond that the trees mark the grounds of the Castro Adobe. (Courtesy ECHS collection.)

50

Herman Rust, the second son of William (Wilhelm) Rust, is pictured behind the family blacksmith shop. Albany Hill is visible in the background. (Courtesy ECHS collection.)

A parade passes the New City Market at the southwest corner of Potrero and San Pablo. Rossi's Athletic Club is in the background. Previously, Rossi had run a winery at this site, until the start of Prohibition in 1920. (Courtesy ECHS collection.)

The first public library in El Cerrito (Rust) opened in 1913. From 1913 until 1950, the library was operated by Fay Breneman, the daughter of Dr. Joseph T. Breneman. The library's first home was in the post office, where Postmaster Barber let Miss Breneman store 50 books . It was open after school three days a week. In 1915, the library moved to a room (above picture) in the Breneman's house. In 1925, the El Cerrito Improvement Association outfitted a space for the library in a building on Fairmount Avenue near Liberty Street (below). This building had previously been used by Marion and Raymond Boles in their business making mint wafers and also by Edward E. Evans in his business making marble monuments and tombstones. (Above courtesy Friends of the El Cerrito Library, ECHS collection; below courtesy ECHS collection.)

In 1946 (not coincidentally, during the first year members of the "Good Government League" were in office), the City of El Cerrito began a search for expanded quarters for the library. In 1949, a new library opened on Stockton Avenue, east of Fairmont School (above picture). It was the first postwar library building in the Bay Area. El Cerrito was growing very rapidly at the time—El Cerrito was the fastest growing city in the East Bay in 1949. In 1959, the voters saw fit to pass a bond issue to enlarge and remodel the existing library. The project was completed in 1960 (below). (Courtesy ECHS collection.)

The Baera family girls pose outside their home near Manila Avenue in El Cerrito. Pictured, from left to right, are Margaret, Inez, Esther, and Edith. The Hutchinson Quarry is visible in the background. (Courtesy Scott family, ECHS collection.)

Another typical El Cerrito family scene from the 1920s, this photograph shows the Nicoli family and their livestock. Many families had some combination of cows, goats, rabbits, and chickens, which they used for milk, eggs, and breeding. From left to right are Mary (in back), Elvira, Louis, John, Frank, and Peter. (Courtesy Nicoli family, ECHS collection.)

A carefree Maria
Mayeda, daughter
of one of the many
Japanese nurserymen
in the El Cerrito
and Richmond area,
stands in a field near
her house on Wall
Avenue. Note how
bare the hills behind
her are. (Courtesy
Maida family,
ECHS collection.)

Genevieve Stark,
the first postmistress
of El Cerrito, poses
outside of the family
home. (Courtesy
Laughlin family,
ECHS collection.)

John Grondona standing in front of his store, Farmers Produce Market. It was north of the Griffin lumberyard and just south of Madison Avenue. The building is the former Panama Pacific Saloon, which was owned by Mr. Camezind and burned down in 1925. (Courtesy ECHS collection.)

Pictured is the bar inside the Grand Central building, 1585 San Pablo Avenue at the corner of Potrero Avenue. From left to right are John Morotti, Harry Bossi, Joe Morotti, unidentified, Rose Poloni, and Josephine Bain. (Courtesy ECHS collection.)

The Central Grocery store at Central and Yosemite Avenues was a fixture in the area for a number of years. It was run by Serafino Chiovaro, who had a store at this location both before and after he ran the Annex Grocery at Panama and San Pablo Avenues. (Courtesy Hansen family, ECHS collection.)

The Central Meat Market at 1527 San Pablo Avenue between Cypress and Potrero Avenues was run by Rose and Louis Poloni, who also had a store in Richmond. Pictured are Francis Gasparini (left) and Louis Poloni. (Courtesy ECHS collection.)

In the 1910s and early 1920s, there was an unimproved landing strip near the county line in El Cerrito, just south of where Harding School stands today. It was a grass field with a few rudimentary markers for pilots. Its key characteristics were that the area was wide-open and relatively flat, which made it quite suitable for the aircraft of that era. (Courtesy Walden family, ECHS collection.)

A long string of aircraft innovations was created by Peter Allinio in the basement and rear yard of his home at 609 Kearney Street. This view is looking northeast. Pictured, from left to right, are Peter Allinio, Pierre Allinio, Marguerite Allinio, and Frank Riley. In October of 1930, Jimmy Angel and Pierre flew this five-place plane to Burbank, California, where they entered it in an endurance flight. (Courtesy Allinio family, ECHS collection.)

At Silas Christofferson Field in Redwood City, (from left to right) Peter Allinio, Pierre Allinio, John Allinio, and Billy Parker enjoy a day of flying. (Courtesy Allinio family, ECHS collection.)

Motorcycle hill climbing competitions on "Peralta Hill" (east of Navellier and Blake Streets) were a regular event in El Cerrito and quite popular. Here an Oakland Motorcycle Club hill climb is in progress. (Courtesy ECHS collection.)

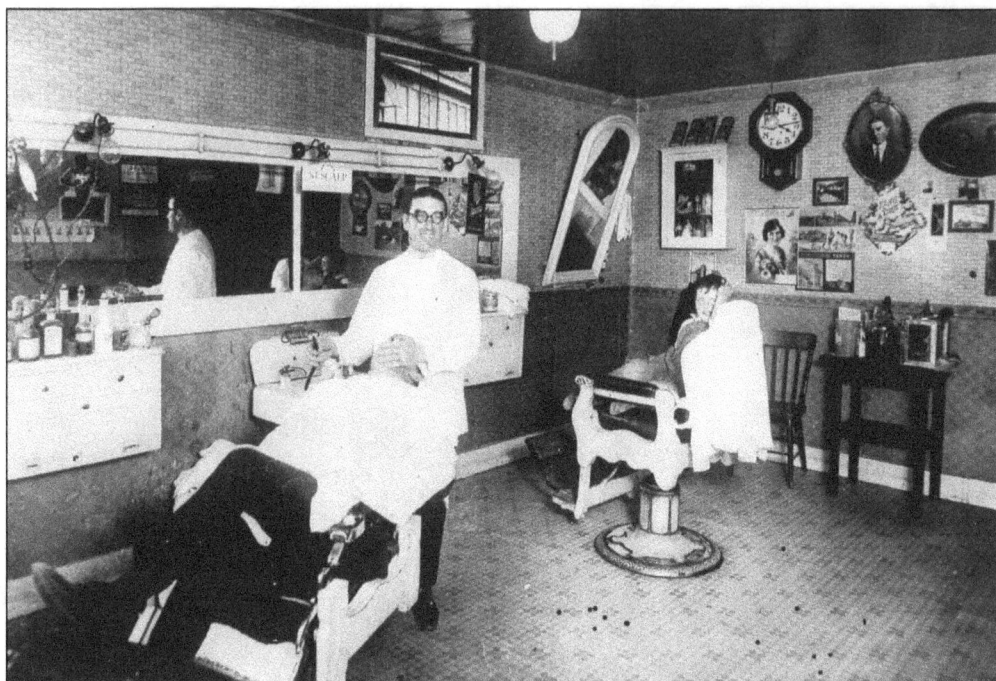

Bert's Barber Shop at 1579 San Pablo Avenue was moved later by Bert farther south on San Pablo and renamed Hollywood Barbers. Bert (Frandio Bortolotti) is giving a customer a shave. Notice the old-fashioned tile floor. (Courtesy ECHS collection.)

Ramon and Baydon Kristavich at their "Twins" service station, looking south down San Pablo Avenue at Cutting Boulevard. Bardon's Fruit Market is just south. The Economy Market and Betsy's Barbeque are across the street, with the Peek-a-Boo Auto Camp in the background. (Courtesy ECHS collection.)

El Cerrito Consumers Supply, run by C. E. Bagley, was on the lower floor of the Rust building, on San Pablo Avenue near Fairmount Avenue. Pictured, from left to right, are Roy Dahlen, Mrs. Christine Batten, and Mrs. Shoute. The boy is Don Batten. (Courtesy ECHS collection.)

Josephine Morotti Bain (left) and John Morotti worked inside the Grand Central building at 1585 San Pablo Avenue, on the corner of Potrero Avenue. (Courtesy ECHS collection.)

The new El Cerrito Fire Department is pictured shortly after the 1926 dedication of the building. From left to right are (first row) ? McMichael, Bill McNalley, Bill Porter, Herman Schwartz, Clayton Morrill, Claude Wheeler, Frank Walsh (ECPD), Chief William Hinds, and Capt. Al Reid; (second row, on the truck) Charles Ellsworth, ? Dietz, Arthur Byrd (driver), Jim Story, and Constable Forrest Wright. (Courtesy ECHS collection.)

Before the Community Methodist Church (pictured) was built on Stockton Avenue, its predecessor, a small building in the 500 block of Richmond Street, was El Cerrito's first church. The original church and Sunday school were founded in 1906 by the Trinity Methodist Church in Berkeley and guided by members of the Berkeley and Oakland churches. (Courtesy ECHS collection.)

Up the hill near Navellier Street and Mound Avenue was the location of the property owned by the Renkwitz family and their descendents, the Reineckers. Here they had a ranch on which they raised hundreds of chickens. The Renkwitzs were the first residents in this part of town. (Courtesy Lent family, ECHS collection.)

The view looking down the hill the from Reinecker property, near the corner of Mound Avenue and Navellier Street shows the creek that ran through the Reinecker property in the foreground. To the right of the trees is the Berkeley Smith Dairy, which was on Gladys Avenue between Everett and Norvell Streets. (Courtesy ECHS collection.)

Back in the days before telephones, fires were reported via an alarm box, a number of which were conveniently located throughout town. The firemen came to the call box, where the person who sounded the alarm would be waiting to direct them to the fire. (Courtesy ECHS collection.)

EL CERRITO FIRE DEPT.
Whist Score Card

Name. *Francesca B.*

Date. *Jan.* *1929.*

Six	*14*	**7**
5	*19*	**8**
4	*17*	**Nine**
3	*23*	**10**
2	*70*	**11**
1		**12**
0		**13**

Total——

Independent Print Shop
Social and Commercial Printing
PROCESS ENGRAVING
Ph ꞏe Richmond 1700   1017 Macdonald Avenue

Before television, card games were a very popular family and social activity. In the 1920s and 1930s, a card game named "whist" was extremely popular and tournaments were held for all age groups, either as a pure competition or as fund-raisers. This is an example of a whist scorecard. (Courtesy ECHS collection.)

Tom Jones, a descendent of Berkeley Smith, rides a raft in the creek that ran down from the Reinecker property. He must be a very experienced rafter because, judging by his shirt and pants, he is in his school clothes and won't be able to sit down for a long time if he comes home soaked. (Courtesy Johnson family, ECHS collection.)

The Stark family poses outside their house, which was just across Moeser Lane from the Bates and Borland rock crusher. From left to right are (first row) Herman, Karolina, Joseph and Josephine. Back Row: Florian, Genevieve, and Thurston. (Courtesy Johnson family, ECHS collection.)

At the Bates and Borland Quarry above today's Arlington Park, a fully loaded rock car is ready for the short run to the transfer station. There the car will dump its load into the top of a bunker. At the bottom of the bunker, the rock is dumped into a funicular railway car for the trip down the tramway to the crusher, at the site of today's Cerrito Vista Park. There are two cars in the system, attached to each other by a cable. As the loaded car descends, the cable system simultaneously pulls an empty car up to the transfer station. Quarry workers occasionally rode the cars down to the crusher instead of walking, and it was said to be a wild ride. (Courtesy Johnson family, ECHS collection.)

This great view of the bottom end of the tramway shows the conveyors, crusher, and bunkers of the Bates and Borland Quarry. This view is from about the intersection of today's Avis Drive and Hotchkiss Avenue. The bunkers and tramway were demolished in 1930 by Vic Belfils and Sam Long. (Courtesy ECHS collection.)

There were a number of dairies in El Cerrito over the years, and here we see part of the herd that belonged to the Mello family, who ran the Stege Dairy on Blake Street and was associated with several other dairies in the area over the years. From left to right are Joe Mello Jr., Joe Mello, Felica Mello, and Alfred Mello. (Courtesy Mello family, ECHS collection.)

A half block north of the Miami Club at Blake Street and San Pablo Avenue, Carl Hansen bought some of the property of the old Lafayette Park. There he opened the Peek-a-Boo Auto Camp, offering campgrounds and cabin rentals. He also had a gas station with two pumps at the corner. North of the corner he had a building that included (as it says on the building) a sandwich shop, a restaurant specializing in chicken dinners, and a dance hall where there was an orchestra every Saturday night. The Peek-a-Boo was surrounded by eucalyptus trees, which were cut down to remodel the grounds into a trailer park. (Courtesy ECHS collection.)

Looking east across San Pablo Avenue from the corner of Lassen Avenue, from left to right, the shops are (first building) the Mechanics Bank and a fountain; (second building) a real estate office, a shoe repair shop, a beauty shop, and William F. Huber's law office. Streetcar tracks are barely visible on San Pablo Avenue. (Courtesy Huber family, ECHS collection.)

Pictured, from left to right, are Charles Sanford, George Sanford, and Mr. Weiss. They bought the building at Manila and San Pablo in 1923 from the Burg brothers (who had a furniture manufacturing company there for a short time). Between 1923 and 1926, it was used as a sheet metal shop, employing between 8 and 16 men and up to seven trucks. The building was later remodeled and served as the city hall starting in 1940. (Courtesy ECHS collection.)

St. John's Catholic church is pictured on the day it was dedicated, February 13, 1927. Quite a fleet of modern vehicles is parked outside. (Courtesy ECHS collection.)

It has been a snowy day in El Cerrito in 1926, and someone has had the foresight to get their camera out so they can prove to their relatives back east how harsh the winters are in the Bay Area. This house still stands on Norvell Street, between Central and Lincoln Avenues. (Courtesy Bootman family, ECHS collection.)

Five

1930–1939

The Hisajiro Honda family poses in one of the hothouses on Potrero Avenue where they grew carnations. From left to right are Sue Honda, Hisajiro Honda, Masue Honda, May Honda, Sachiko Honda, and Jun Honda. (Courtesy Honda family, ECHS collection.)

The 1936 Louis Hagen Post 340 American Legion Baseball Junior team, pictured at Harding School, included, from left to right, ? Pemberton, Steve Welch, Howard Buell, ? Chase, Darrel Salmon, Shirley Weeks, Elmo Nicoli, Al Blase, Johnnie Mewha, and Clyde Gillam. (Courtesy ECHS collection.)

The El Cerrito Fire Department baseball team included, from left to right, (first row) Ed Gagnon, ? Corriea, Al Baxter, Marcus ?, Glen Bullard, and Vic Belfils; (second row) Jack Pinto, George Weeks, ? Hastings, Jack O'Connell, S. S. Hudson, and Don Bonini. (Courtesy ECHS collection.)

Story Time in the children's section of the library has always been a favorite among the younger patrons of the library. Here Librarian Ruth Colburn entertains a large crowd. (Courtesy Friends of the El Cerrito Library, ECHS collection.)

The parade up Fink Lane (now Portola Drive) to St. John's Hall during the annual "Holy Ghost" festival was a special observance for Portuguese Catholics. The parade was between St. John's church on San Pablo Avenue and St. John's Hall on Fink Lane. The original route used San Pablo Avenue, but in later years it was shifted to Richmond Street. Services were held at the church, and then there was a feast (featuring *sopas*) at St. John's Hall. Judge Huber is the man in the dark suit on the sidewalk. (Courtesy ECHS collection.)

The Grand Central Store at the southwest corner of Potrero and San Pablo Avenues was next door to a branch of the Mechanics Bank. Note the overhead wire for the streetcar line. (Courtesy Poloni family, ECHS collection.)

Some true El Cerrito pioneers celebrate Mother's Day in 1934. From left to right are Katherine (Sullivan) Hagen (1864–1948), Louis C. Hagen (1860–1950), and Blanche Brodt (1885–1964). Katie A. Hagen was the daughter of Patrick Sullivan, who came west in the 1860s and settled in Wildcat Canyon. Louis C. Hagen, son of Chris Hagen, was born on December 13, 1860, where Sunset View Cemetery is now located. Blanche Brodt was the daughter of Louis and Katie. Their son Louis C. Hagen was killed in the Battle for the Marne during World War I. The American Legion Post in El Cerrito is named in his honor. (Courtesy ECHS collection.)

Louis and Frank Nicoli pose inside Nicoli's Market on the east side of San Pablo Avenue, just south of Moeser Lane. (Courtesy Nicoli family, ECHS collection.)

Here is the original factory of the Technical Porcelain and Chinaware Company on Manila Avenue, owned and run by John Pagliero and his family. They produced a well-known line of durable and distinctive chinaware products from the 1930s to the 1960s. For many years "TEPCO" was the largest employer in El Cerrito. This factory burned down in 1946 and was replaced by a new and larger factory, which was eventually razed and replaced by the Department of Motor Vehicles building on Manila Avenue. (Courtesy ECHS collection.)

Sunset View Cemetery at the top of Fairmount Avenue was founded in 1908. The original gated entrance to the cemetery (above) was built around 1920. Note the almost complete absence of trees in this area. The waterfall was built in the 1930s. (Both courtesy of Sunset View Cemetery, ECHS collection.)

Pictured at El Cerrito Fire Department Station No. 1, San Pablo and Manila Avenues, from left to right, are (first row) Patterson, Tezzi, Long, Gagnon, Lewis, Phief, Baxter, Burnett, H. Richardson, D. Bonini, and R. Richardson; (second row) S. S. Hudson, V. Belfils, Riley, E. Belfils, Wilson, Herman, L. Richardson, M. Belfils, and Hammond. (Courtesy ECHS collection.)

From left to right, driver Victor Belfils, Mike Duncan, and Chief Ora Burnetta were on hand to dedicate this new Chevrolet fire truck at Fire Station No. 1 on San Pablo and Manila Avenues. (Courtesy ECHS collection.)

Dogs and their grooms are at the ready on the track at the El Cerrito Kennel Club, operated by John J. "Blackjack" Jerome. Construction was started on the Kennel Club in September 1932 by the Wembly Amusement Corporation. The Kennel Club closed down in 1939 after its license was revoked. The grandstand was demolished May 10, 1948, and a drive-in theater replaced it. Pictured, from left to right, are Harry Lutz, Walter Gatto, Ray Lutz, George Weeks, Al Varallo, Erwin Marcos, Eldon Gilbert, Don Bonini, Al Wilson, and Horace Mots. (Courtesy ECHS collection.)

This is a November 19, 1934, cover of a typical day's racing program at the Kennel Club. (Courtesy ECHS collection.)

Construction of the grandstand and track at the El Cerrito Kennel Club was started September, 1932. This picture is believed to have been taken before the track opened to the public. Harding School is near the center of the photograph, and the Sunset View Cemetery and the Sunset Mausoleum building are directly above it. At the left center of the photograph are the farm buildings originally erected for John Balra's dairy. (Courtesy ECHS collection.)

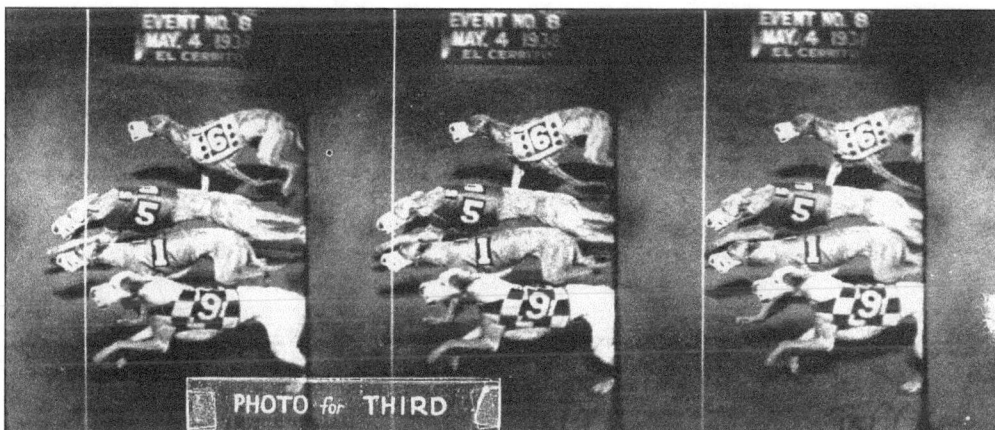

A "Photo Finish" at the dog track. Note how the different muzzles worn by the dogs helped make the order of finish easier to discern in close races such as this one. (Courtesy ECHS collection.)

These are typical 1932 grocery advertisements from New City Market (San Pablo and Potrero Avenues) and the El Nido Market. The ads commemorate the opening of the Veterans Memorial Building. The address of the New City Market is from the "old" numbering scheme. In the 1950s, all the cities along San Pablo Avenue decided to renumber the street so that addresses along San Pablo Avenue would ascend uniformly as one traveled north from downtown Oakland. However, an examination of today's addresses on San Pablo Avenue reveals that not all the cities followed up their words with deeds. (Courtesy ECHS collection.)

In the years following World War I, thousands of Veterans Memorial Buildings were constructed across America. The Louis Hagen Post of the American Legion made an application for a memorial building in El Cerrito to the county board of supervisors and was granted the sum of $22,500 to purchase the site and construct the building. The dedication of the new building in 1932 was one of the largest such affairs held in El Cerrito up to that date. The featured event was a big parade down San Pablo Avenue from Cutting Boulevard to Stockton Avenue and then up Stockton to the new building. It was one of the first memorial buildings in the county that could be used by the entire community and its organizations. (Courtesy Panas family, ECHS collection.)

A CORDIAL INVITATION IS EXTENDED TO YOURSELF
AND YOUR FRIENDS TO ATTEND THE

DEDICATION EXERCISES

OF THE

EL CERRITO VETERANS MEMORIAL BUILDING
EL CERRITO, CALIFORNIA
LOCATED AT CORNER OF STOCKTON AVENUE AND KEARNY STREET

SATURDAY AFTERNOON, SEPETEMBER 24, 1932 AT 2:30

THE EXERCISES WILL BE HELD UNDER THE AUSPICES OF

LOUIS HAGEN POST No. 340, AMERICAN LEGION
DEPARTMENT OF CALIFORNIA

EL CERRITO POST No. 2521, VETERANS OF FOREIGN WARS
DEPARTMENT OF CALIFORNIA AND NEVADA

The dedication of the new Veterans Memorial Building took place September 24, 1932. The American Legion post was named for Louis Hagen, the descendent of an El Cerrito pioneer. He was killed in action in France during World War I. (Courtesy ECHS collection.)

This view of El Cerrito from Albany Hill looks out over Adams Street and San Pablo Avenue toward El Cerrito. The Victor Castro Adobe is in the grove of large eucalyptus trees near the center of the picture. The large building near the top of the hill at the right of the photograph is the Sunset Mausoleum building. (Courtesy ECHS collection.)

From left to right in front of city hall, E.C. Police Department officer Art Peralta, police chief R. R. Cheek, and fire chief O. A. Burnett are about to break up 18 barrels of wine seized during Prohibition. The arresting officer was Art Peralta. El Cerrito was notorious for bootlegging and gambling in those days, and it is amazing to consider how infrequently illegal alcohol was seized. (Courtesy ECHS collection.)

Six

1940–1949

El Cerrito High has not been expanded yet in this view looking southeast toward El Cerrito High and Albany Hill from Balra Drive. Beyond El Cerrito High, the grandstand of the long-gone dog track and the trailers that occupied the race track area during the war are visible. (Courtesy ECHS collection.)

The Roberre Lelieux House was a landmark for many years at 611 Lexington Avenue, just north of Lincoln Avenue. It was referred to as the "Castle" by those who admired it and the "Haunted House" by the young children who had to walk by it (or who went out of their way to avoid walking by it) on their way to or from school, the store, or the movies. It was only a block east from another well-known house in El Cerrito, Peter Allinio's residence at 609 Kearney Street. (Courtesy Bray family, ECHS collection.)

The Girl's Club in El Cerrito was located at 829 Norvell Street. The City of El Cerrito acquired the property from Veronica Davis in 1939 for $85. In 1942, the Girls Club Association was formed and one of the Breneman daughters, Hazel, was the secretary. The clubhouse was built entirely with volunteer labor and with donated materials and funds. In 1959 the "Hill & Dale" Women's Club sponsored a 1,000-square-foot addition to the facility to meet the needs of senior citizens who were using the facility by this time. (Courtesy ECHS collection.)

This view looks north on San Pablo Avenue from Fairmount Avenue in 1948. Jack Vier's Chevron station stood at the corner, and Log Cabin Bakery, Smart Cleaners, Dill's Drugstore, and more stores lined the street. Just visible on the left side of San Pablo Avenue is the sign for the Six Bells bar and restaurant. (Courtesy ECHS collection.)

On April 1, 1943, the El Cerrito Trailer Court opened, with 250 units ready for occupancy. Wartime housing was in extremely short supply, and it was estimated that approximately 2,000 people would be accommodated in this 666-unit trailer court. The rental for trailer applicants was set at $4 per week. This trailer court was constructed on a portion of the old El Cerrito Kennel Club site. Part of the old grandstand of the Kennel Club can be seen at the right in this picture. The grandstand was finally demolished in 1948. This view is from the north side of Fairmount Avenue, near Liberty Street. (Courtesy ECHS collection.)

OFFICIAL PROGRAM

FIESTA del CERRITO

September 13 to 19 Inclusive

1948

El Cerrito, California

This is the week of Fiesta in historic El Cerrito, California. The City of El Cerrito is your host, and in the traditional spirit of Fiesta we welcome you to join us. The week is filled with events to entertain you. The proceeds of all activities goes to the El Cerrito Youth Foundation, Inc., dedicated to the benefit of the youth of this area.

PRICE 25 CENTS
Tax Included

The "Fiesta del Cerrito" was a city-wide event to celebrate the return home of all the GI's who fought in World War II and also the (roughly) 30th anniversary of the incorporation of El Cerrito. It was a week-long event with many attractions and culminated with a large parade and party. (Courtesy ECHS collection.)

The fiesta parade included this entry from the Young Ladies Institute, a Catholic women's organization. Here the float passes at Central and San Pablo. The sign for the Six Bells Restaurant and Tavern can be seen in the background. From left to right are the following: two unidentified, Carmen Delgado, "Queen" Betty Rose, Mary Ann Osterholtz, and Millie Osterholtz. (Courtesy Lambie family, ECHS collection.)

This float was the Louie's Club entry in the fiesta parade. Louie's Club was a very well-known restaurant and tavern on San Pablo Avenue, north of Potrero Avenue. The photograph was taken just north of Fairmount and San Pablo Avenues. (Courtesy Nicoli family, ECHS collection.)

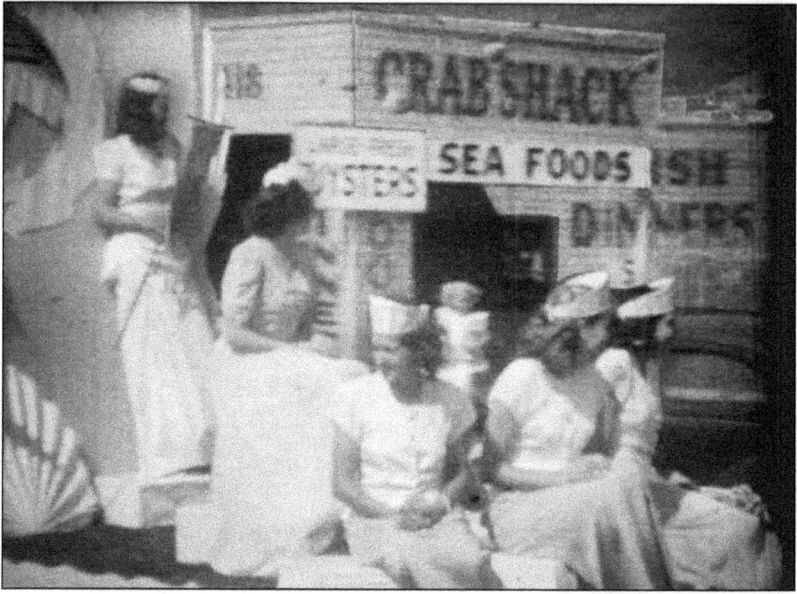

Though a bit blurry, this is a photograph of arguably the most famous "hole in the wall" eatery that ever existed in El Cerrito. John Grondona's Crab Shack was a legend among the locals and remembered vividly by all who ever ate there. The seafood was always fresh, and John's crab was renown. The Crab Shack was on the east side of San Pablo Avenue, just south of Madison Avenue. (Courtesy ECHS collection.)

2101 SAN PABLO AVENUE
corner of Wall Street
EL CERRITO, CALIFORNIA

The first self-service gas station in the Bay Area and reputedly the entire West Coast was at the

Santa Fe's "California Limited" (train No. 4), pulled by two Alco PA locomotives, has just crossed Knott Avenue on the first leg of the voyage to Chicago. Passengers will arrive there in a little less than three days. (Photograph by John Ilman; courtesy ECHS collection.)

SERVE YOURSELF
SAVE a major GASOLINE

"SERVE YOURSELF GASOLINE STATION"
2101 SAN PABLO AVENUE
EL CERRITO, CALIFORNIA

corner of San Pablo Avenue and Wall Avenue. (Courtesy Umbraco family, ECHS collection.)

Volunteer firemen Jim Glasson (left) and Mervin Belfils pilot a fire truck up San Pablo Avenue during the 30th anniversary fiesta. (Courtesy ECHS collection.)

This is El Cerrito High as it appeared when first completed. Looking northwest, the only buildings on the site are the gymnasium, the main classroom building that is parallel to Ashbury Avenue, and the Shop building. (Courtesy Richmond Museum of History.)

The football team at El Cerrito High originally played its games at a field built on the site of the dog track. In the background of this image are the house trailers that occupied most of the El Cerrito Plaza area during the war. Identifiable players include Ed Rodriguez (no. 4) and quarterback Johnny Waters (no. 13). (Courtesy Enz family, ECHS collection.)

Here is the El Cerrito 30th anniversary fiesta parade on San Pablo Avenue between Central and Fairmount Avenues. The driver of the fire truck (which was called "Old Betsy") is Jim Glasson. Next to him is volunteer chief Mervin Belfils. Al Lewis is on top of the truck. (Courtesy ECHS collection.)

In this c. 1941 aerial view of El Cerrito, the three original buildings at El Cerrito High are visible. Moeser Lane ends at Navellier Street, and many of today's structures, including Portola Middle School (built in 1951), are missing. Even in the "filled-in" part of town there are many lots without houses. A trailer park for wartime employees occupies the site of today's El Cerrito Plaza, and there is a boxcar on the Santa Fe spur at Fairmount Avenue. (Courtesy ECHS collection.)

This photograph looks up Schmidt Lane from Navellier Street at the Hutchinson Quarry bunkers. This building will soon meet its fate as a training site for the El Cerrito Fire Department. (Courtesy ECHS collection.)

This building was constructed by Mr. Copperburger and leased to Denny Sullivan, who ran it as a saloon named "Sullivan's." Joseph Jacobs bought it in 1914 and remodeled it as a dance hall, saloon, and restaurant. He named it the "Miami Club" and catered to a somewhat elite clientele. After his death, a new attraction was added on the second floor—prostitution. Shortly before World War II, Angelo Fara, who started Angelo's Market, bought the building. In 1944, Joe and Vincent DeMartini leased and operated it until 1949. Soon afterward, the building was demolished. (Courtesy ECHS collection.)

COMMUNISTS SEEK TO CONTROL EL CERRITO

The Communist party was re... ...day as a prime factor seeking the recall of Mayor Louis E. Da... ...d Councilmen Edward L. Smith and ... ...t tomorrow's municipal election in El Cerrito.

The People's Daily ... ...per, lifted the smoke-screen in a last minute distribu... certain secti... ...

"The ... ...ement," a feature article bluntly stated.

...naires and members of the El Cerrito P... ...ght to organize full strength to defeat th... ...rnment.

...gen Post of the American Legion in El Cer... ...r urging a vote "Yes" on the recall under t... ...rs, 358 South 50th Street, Richmond. (We...

..."George Kauffmann, staff writer."

...ague, is prominently mentioned in the Commun... ...ies in the recall, and his residence at 411 Clayton ...

...Communist. Records show ...tatement:

Good Government Puts Three More Members On El Cerrito Council

Citizens Group Consolidates To Institute Recall Action Against Davis — Smith — Cisi

The Poor Taxpayer

Large Vote Anticipated Wednesday

City Recall, Council Election on Tuesday

Cerrito Set For Special City Election

Free Rides to Polling Places Wednesday

One Light Enough. Commy Dam...

VETER...

COUNCILMEN IN EL CERRITO OUSTED

Bostock, Heinkel Win

Recalled

Good Gov't League Is Disbanded

In 1945, a group of citizens who wanted to be proud of the city in which they lived and who wanted to create a desirable place to raise families formed a group known as the Good Government League. They adopted the slogan "The City of Homes" and then set about to build a city that would live up to that slogan. The Good Government League—campaigning on a platform of clean, efficient government—was successful in recalling three city council members and electing an entirely new city council. The headlines indicate that the election was a bit rancorous. (Courtesy ECHS collection.)

The Chung Mei Home ("Chinese American") opened June 30, 1935, at the intersection of Hill and Elm Streets. It was a home for abandoned Chinese boys. Those who were raised there were highly disciplined, motivated, and hard working. In fact, through the proceeds from their wood yard and their musical performances, they paid for the 5.5-acre plot that the Chung Mei home was built upon, plus part of the construction cost. (Courtesy ECHS collection.)

These interior and exterior photographs clearly show the style and detail that went into the design and construction of the Chung Mei Home. It's hard to believe that it was entirely financed by donations from the community and the money the boys earned. The home was originally located in an old wooden building in West Berkeley, which it soon outgrew. After it closed, the home was turned over to the Western Baptist Bible College and then later became Armstrong Preparatory School. Today it is the campus of the Windrush School. (Courtesy ECHS collection.)

This postwar and pre-freeway view is from the Honda family's house on the grounds of their nursery, which fronted on Eastshore and Potrero Avenues. Visible beyond the western edge of the nursery is a small part of the housing built during World War II to accommodate the war workers, who between 1941 and 1945 swelled Richmond's population from 25,000 to 100,000. (Courtesy Honda family, ECHS collection.)

The back side of this piece of TEPCO China shows the address of the main plant and the branch offices. (Courtesy Panas family, ECHS collection.)

Seven

1950–1959.

The 1958 city council included Doris Hormel, who became the first female mayor of El Cerrito. She was a popular mayor and a force to be reckoned with during her years on the city council. Pictured, from left to right, are Leo Armstrong, John Conway, Doris Hormel, Charles Apple, and Henry Gillan. (Courtesy ECHS collection.)

This is the overgrown Castro Adobe as it looked the day before it burned to the ground (April 20, 1956). It had been the home of Victor Castro from 1839 to 1900. (Courtesy Ross family, ECHS collection.)

Very little remains of the Castro Adobe after the fire that burned it down in 1956. (Courtesy Ringbom family, ECHS collection.)

Above is another view of the sad remains of the Castro Adobe several days after the fire that destroyed it in 1956. The photograph below shows the desolate remnants of El Cerrito's drive-in theater that was located on the land formerly occupied by the dog track and today occupied by the El Cerrito Plaza shopping center. The drive-in was built in 1948 and remained open until the mid-1950s. (Above photograph courtesy Ringbom family, ECHS collection; photograph below courtesy ECHS collection.)

The 1950 El Cerrito Elementary Championship Basketball team (from Castro School) and three members of the Junior High championship team (from Portola) are, from left to right, (front row) Bill Wong, Tom Lin, Mickey Chung, Victor Wong, and Wing Tom; (back row) Jules Voerge, Lowie Whitlock, and Jim Grisham. (Courtesy ECHS collection.)

Some of the entrants in the annual Bike Day contest wait on the playground at Fairmont School. The Veterans Memorial Building is visible beyond the playground, across Stockton Avenue. (Courtesy ECHS collection.)

A newspaper recycling drive is on, and the team from the Catacombs Club has collected quite a pile. The Catacombs Club was a recreation center and pool built and supported by St. John's Catholic church. It was on the east side of the Santa Fe tracks, between Donal and Gladys Avenues. Ernie Broglio is in the dark jacket with the turned-up collar. (Courtesy Nordahl family, ECHS collection.)

This is the front entrance to the clubhouse at Mira Vista Golf and Country Club, originally incorporated in 1920 as the Berkeley Country Club. The clubhouse was designed by W. H. Radcliffe and built in 1921. The course originally had 9 holes, but plans were soon made to add holes 10 through 18. (Courtesy ECHS collection.)

These hothouses were on John Belliardo's nursery between Schmidt Lane and Fink Lane (now Portola Drive), where several other nurseries of Italian growers were located, including those of the DeMartinis, the Figones, and the Farinas. The nurseries were all east of the Santa Fe tracks, and some were in the path of Richmond Street, which did not go through between Moeser and Schmidt Lanes until the 1950s. (Courtesy Belliardo family, ECHS collection.)

Mayor Doris Hormel cuts the ribbon during the dedication ceremonies for the new El Cerrito Plaza shopping center, assisted by, from left to right, Robert D. Fraser (chairman of the developer), Blair Burton (master of ceremonies), Don L. Kimball (in charge of the fiesta), Les Brown (chamber of commerce president), and O.G. Battershill (also from the chamber of commerce). Surrounding them are fiesta-queen hopefuls. (Courtesy ECHS collection.)

Fire chief Ora Burnett dispenses some fireworks safety advice to a group of cub scouts who are hoping to make a big bang on July 4th. (Courtesy ECHS collection.)

This aerial view shows the state of development in El Cerrito in the 1950s. El Cerrito Plaza is prominent, as is the former Hutchinson Quarry. About the only large area still undeveloped is the hillside area north of the quarry. (Courtesy ECHS collection.)

The view looking north from Stockton and San Pablo Avenues shows a striking maze of utility poles and wires. Only the Bank of America is still in the same location. This part of San Pablo Avenue became part of the first assessment district for street lighting and undergrounding of utilities in El Cerrito. Note the U.S. Highway 40 sign; currently there is a movement afoot to re-sign the entire original route of U.S. Highway 40 as "Historic Route 40." (Courtesy ECHS collection.)

The Boys Club building stands on the far side of the baseball diamond at Cerrito Vista Park. The community center on Moeser Lane has not yet been built. Interesting to note are the power poles going out to Brooks Island and also the large incinerator at El Cerrito Mill and Lumber, near the foot of Schmidt lane. (Courtesy ECHS collection.)

Eight

1960–1969

Pictured is the Breneman house at 10135 San Pablo Avenue, the day the building was demolished. It was built in 1914 by Dr. Joseph T. Breneman. Two of the Breneman daughters, Hazel and Fay, lived in the house until the day before it was demolished in 1963. The house was used for a period by Dr. Breneman as his office and for 10 years one room in the house served as the area's library. (Courtesy ECHS collection.)

This is the view south along San Pablo Avenue from the northern border of town. The population of El Cerrito has dropped a bit (23,171 in the 2000 Census) since those years. The Adachi nursery is visible on the right, as well as a Norwalk gas station. (Courtesy Odlin family, ECHS collection.)

The El Cerrito City Hall Building was in use from 1940 until 1987, when it was demolished due to earthquake survivability issues. At that time, the city offices relocated into "temporary" portable buildings, which 18 years later are still in use. (Courtesy ECHS collection.)

This was the view west from the intersection of Fairmount and San Pablo Avenues, before Fairmount Avenue was put through to Carlson Blvd in the early 1960s. At that time, the Kiefer Furniture store moved to the corner of Central and San Pablo Avenues, where it remained for more than 40 years. The buildings on the west side of San Pablo Avenue were once owned by the Rusts. Note the Doggie Diner at the corner of Lassen and San Pablo. (Courtesy ECHS collection.)

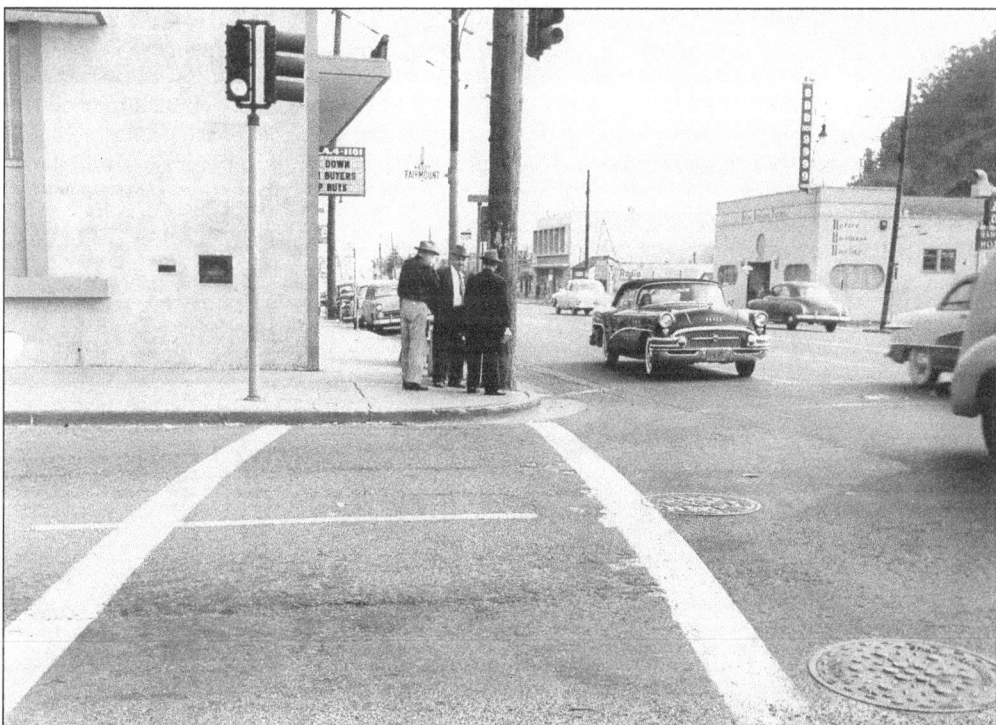

A view south from Fairmount and San Pablo Avenues shows the Mechanics Bank building on the left. The Doggie Diner is just visible across San Pablo Avenue. Bill Pechart's "Citadel," where enormous amounts of money changed hands (mostly into Bill's) in earlier days, is a bit further down the avenue. (Courtesy Odlin family, ECHS collection.)

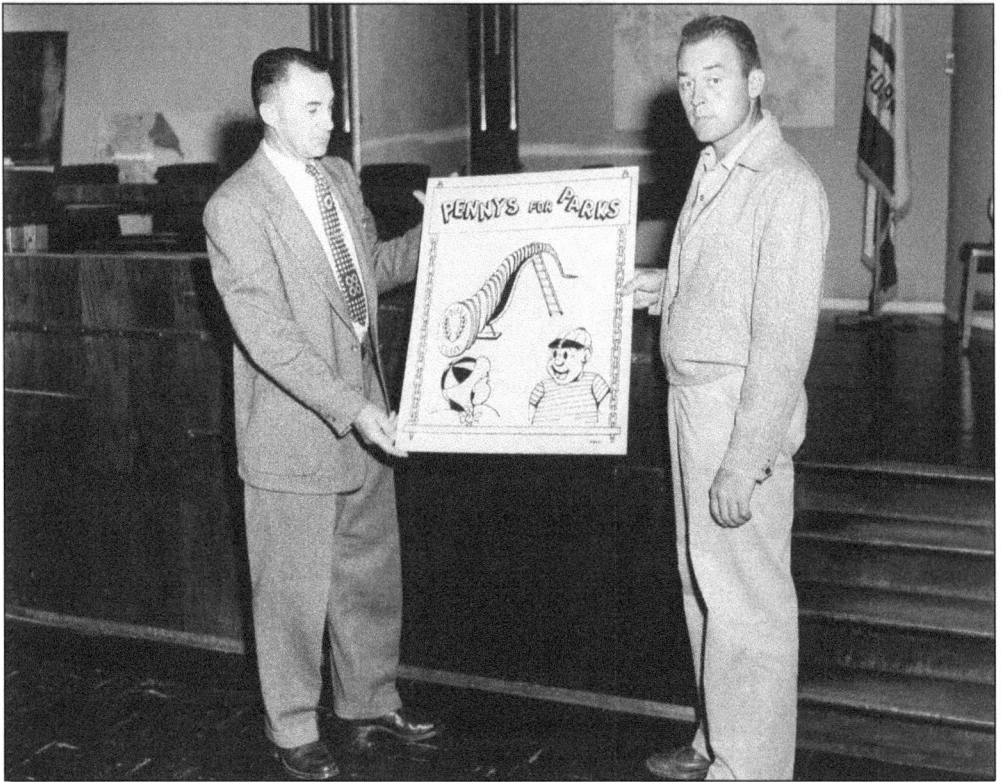

The "Pennies for Parks" bond issue was put on the ballot by the 1964 city council to fund the purchase of land for several new parks and the development at a number of others. It passed and made possible many of the parks that we take for granted in El Cerrito today. Here Councilman Edward A. Valentino (left) and an unidentified man hold one of the publicity signs for the election. (Courtesy ECHS collection.)

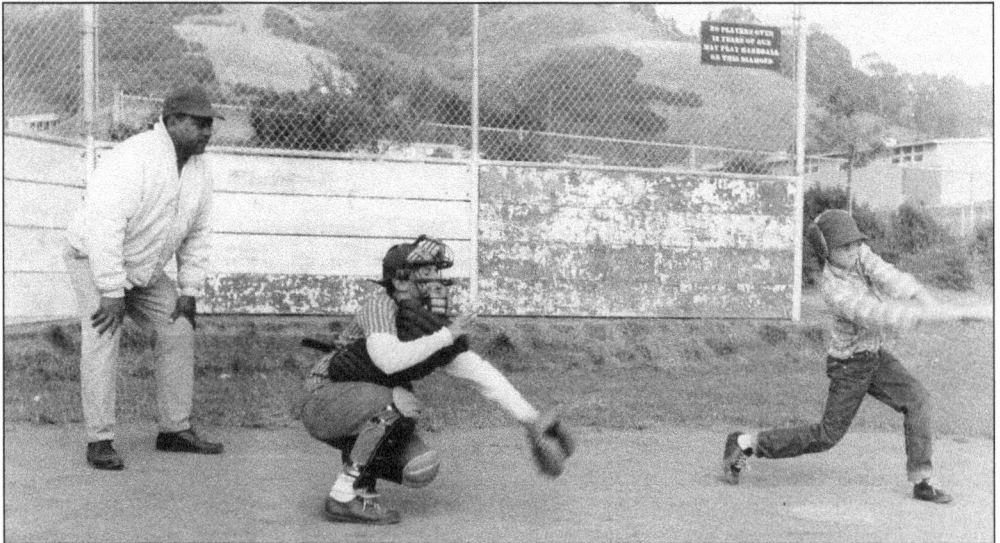

This picture is one of the publicity shots taken for the Pennies for Parks bond issue campaign. (Courtesy ECHS collection.)

Three happy children enjoy the circular slide at Cerrito Vista Park in another publicity photograph taken for the Pennies for Parks bond issue. (Courtesy ECHS collection.)

The students at Madera School register their enthusiasm for the news that the Pennies for Parks bond issue passed. The Pennies for Parks program was one of the last projects taken on by the group of people who initially constituted the Good Government League in 1945. (Courtesy ECHS collection.)

The winners of El Cerrito Recreation Department Athletic Achievement awards pose with their plaques. Before the budget cutbacks that resulted from Proposition 13, El Cerrito had a large and very busy recreation program serving children all over the city. Pictured, from left to right, are (first row) Judy Hollingshead, Sharon Schaefer, and Ione Olson; (second row) Charles Garagg, Spike Dobbins, and Steve Prudhomme. (Courtesy ECHS collection.)

El Cerrito Building Supply, a cement and building materials business, was located where the El Cerrito Plaza BART station stands today. Here part of the main building comes down in preparation for BART construction. El Cerrito Plaza is visible in the background. The Santa Fe tracks in the area had to be relocated to make way for BART. (Courtesy ECHS collection.)

Nine

1970–1979

The El Cerrito City Club was an institution for many years in town. It was founded during the beginning of World War II by Louis Navellier, Ira Scott, Clarence Brenzell, and Harry Bossi. Their goal was to raise $50 to give to every serviceman who returned home from the war. They succeeded in this, and entertained and fed busload after busload of servicemen from Oak Knoll Naval Hospital during the war. They originally met weekly at Rossi's on Potrero Avenue, but switched to St. John's Hall after Rossi's burned down. Before the end of 1942, they were in a new building they had erected at Potrero Avenue and Kearney Street. After the war the club became more of a service and social club. A number of service clubs, plus the City of El Cerrito itself, used the facilities at the City Club. It was, of course, a male-only bastion, except during special events. (Courtesy ECHS collection.)

El Cerrito was among the earliest cities nationwide to pursue renewable energy and recycling strategies in the 1970s. The Recycling Center was well-promoted both in the media and by word of mouth. The above photograph shows a recycling billboard in the El Cerrito Del Norte BART station. Below, a sign at the Recycling Center (in those days, it was called "ECology") indicates that the center was founded in 1972. (Both courtesy Ringbom family, ECHS collection.)

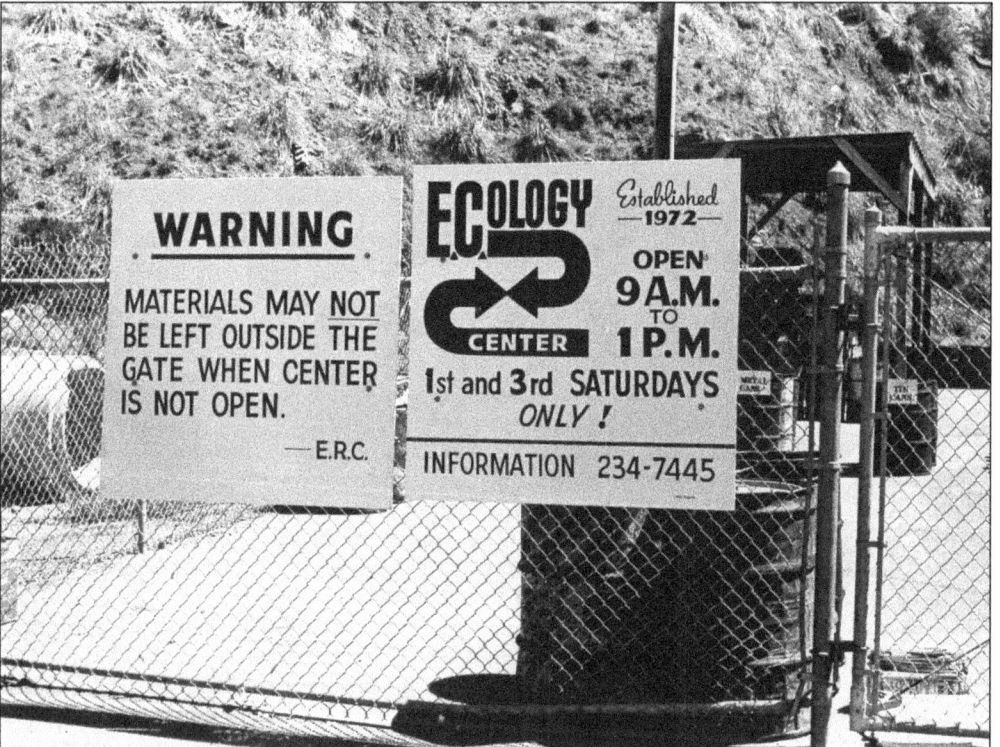

In another example of the city's pursuit of conservation and energy efficiency, the swimming pool at the El Cerrito Community Center was heated using a solar system mounted on the roof of the community center. (Courtesy ECHS collection.)

Once the BART system started operating, attention turned to beautifying the BART corridor. Efforts on this eventually led to today's Ohlone Greenway. In this picture, ground is broken for a demonstration beautification project north of the Del Norte BART station. Pictured, from left to right, are Anna Mascaro, an unidentified HUD representative, two unidentified men, Troy Kitchens, Jim Kenney, and unidentified. (Courtesy ECHS collection.)

Sundar Shadi's summer flower displays in his large garden facing Arlington Avenue, just north of Moeser Lane, were famous. Here Shadi stands in front of the floral arrangement he planted to celebrate the bicentennial. While his summer displays were well known around town, his Christmas displays drew people from all over the East Bay every year. (Courtesy ECHS collection.)

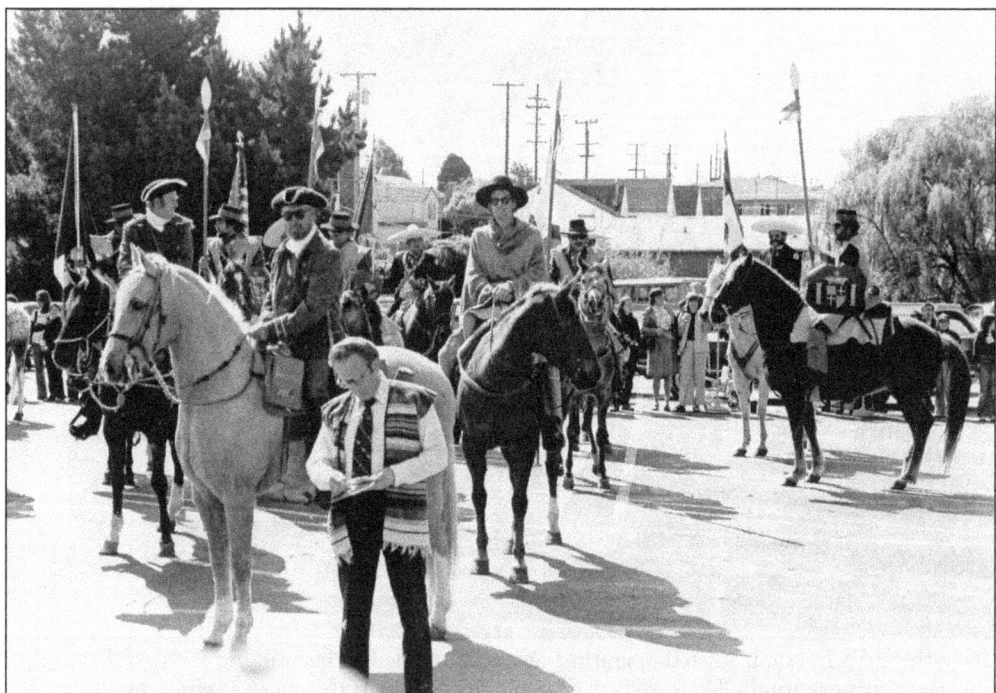

As part of the bicentennial celebration in El Cerrito, a parade was held with people in period costumes. Here participants can be seen wearing both Mexican and Colonial garb. (Courtesy ECHS collection.)

Native Americans left their mark all over El Cerrito, primarily as shell mounds, mortar holes, and rock art. Here Dr. Albert Elsasser from the University of California stands next to a large rock that has a number of depressions made by the native Huchiun Indians. (Courtesy ECHS collection.)

Service clubs have always been an important part of life for many men and women in El Cerrito. The clubs have made many wonderful contributions and improvements to El Cerrito. Here the El Cerrito Fire Department receives a gift from the El Cerrito Rotary Club, "The Jaws of Life." (Courtesy Odlin family, ECHS collection.)

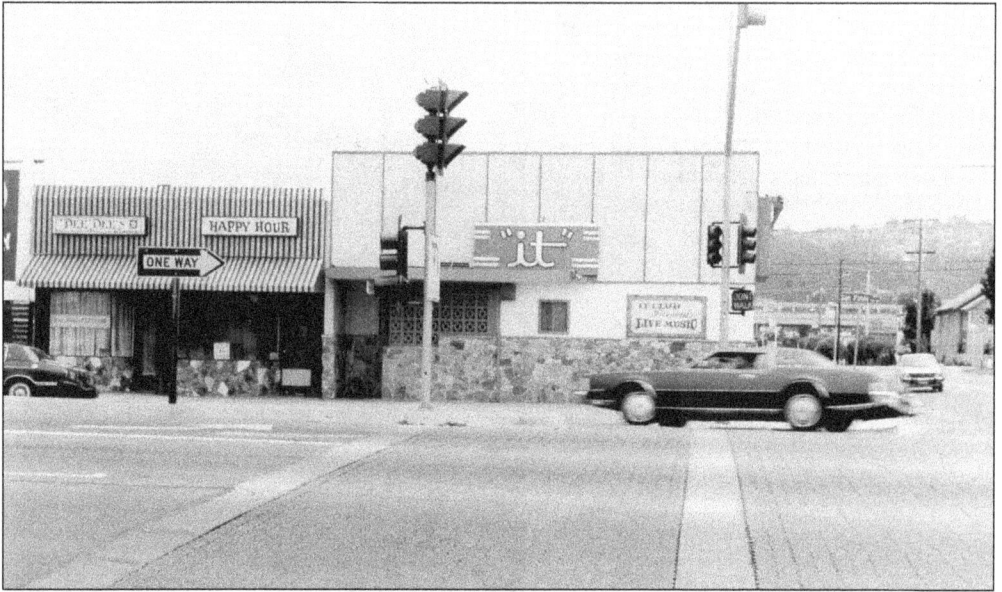

Although never very pretty on the outside, the "it" Club, owned by Walter Gatto, was a very popular music club in El Cerrito. Clara Bow, the famous "It" Girl of the movies, was a personal friend of Mr. Gatto, who named the club after her. Some of the entertainers who performed at the "it" Club were Red Foxx, Gypsy Rose Lee, Sally Rand, The Vagabonds, Frank Fontaine, Johnny Mathis, and many more. Mr. Gatto sold the "it" Club in 1977. (Courtesy Collier family, ECHS collection.)

The Cerrito Theatre was located on the east side of San Pablo Avenue, between Central and Fairmount Avenues. It opened in 1937 and was a joint venture between Henry Goldenberg and the Blumenfield theater chain. The theater had 644 seats, delighting children and entertaining adults until 1966. (Courtesy Kirby family, ECHS collection.)

Ten

1980 AND BEYOND

Still Making History in Local Real Estate

Chelsea Railway Station, Circa 1916

Photograph from Chelsea & District Historical Society Inc
Court House Museum, The Strand, Chelsea. Open Sundays 1 to 4pm, Admission $2.

The City of El Cerrito has had a sister-city relationship with Chelsea, Australia (a suburb of Melbourne) for a number of years. Likewise, the two historical societies have a similar relationship. Here is an image of a postcard promoting the Chelsea Society's museum. The initial contact between the two cities was made by the Chelsea Rotary Club. (Courtesy Chelsea and District Historical Society, ECHS collection.)

In these two images, a number of the buildings at El Cerrito Plaza are being demolished to allow the Plaza to be modernized. Above, on August 29, 2000, the ceremonial "first bite" is taken out of the building that housed the popular Kirbys restaurant. In the photograph below, the east

parking lot has been removed and the old Capwells building has been encased in plastic to do hazardous material abatement prior to razing the building. (Both photographs courtesy Odlin family, ECHS collection.)

The old Capwells building is pictured as it takes its last gasp. Most of the building is gone, but part of the second story has not yet succumbed to the wrecker's ball. The building that houses Longs Drug Store was not demolished as part of the modernization, and is visible at the right. The BART tracks can be seen beyond the remains of Capwells. (Courtesy Duveneck family, ECHS collection.)

It was happy news for all as the revitalized Plaza reopened for business in 2001. The remnants of the old Hutchinson quarry are visible in the distance. (Courtesy Odlin family, ECHS collection.)

The El Cerrito Mill and Lumber retail building, owned for years by the Freethy family, is moved from the east to the west side of San Pablo Avenue. When the El Cerrito Mill and Lumber site was sold and redevelopment plans were announced, a local businessman took it upon himself to save the retail shop. He moved it off the property being redeveloped to a spot across the street, renovated it, and rented out the commercial space. (Courtesy Odlin family, ECHS collection.)

The playhouse and workspace of the Contra Costa Civic Theater have been a part of El Cerrito for more than 45 years. Founded in 1959 by Louis and Bettianne Flynn, the organization was invited in 1970 by the City of El Cerrito to take over the former Boys Club building on Moeser Lane at Pomona. The Contra Costa Civic Theater provides vocal, make-up, lighting, costuming, playwriting, set construction, drama, and musical theater training. (Courtesy Panas family, ECHS collection.)

In the last years of his life, Sundar Shadi was no longer able to set up his famous Christmas display. Fortunately, Soroptimist International of El Cerrito was willing to take over for him. Now they, along with the El Cerrito Foundation, conserve Shadi's artwork and put up the Christmas display each year on Moeser Lane. (Courtesy Duveneck family, ECHS collection.)

Celebrating its 100th anniversary in 2005, the "Regalia House" on San Pablo Avenue serves as a reminder of long-ago times and people in El Cerrito. Ellen Smith Regalia, one of the girls in the pictures on pages 12 and 20, who, as a young girl, moved with her family to El Cerrito in 1897, is one of many to live in this house. (Courtesy Panas family, ECHS collection.)

Visit us at
arcadiapublishing.com

www.ingramcontent.com/pod-product-compliance
Lightning Source LLC
Chambersburg PA
CBHW080625110426
42813CB00006B/1608